NEWGRANGE, DOWTH & KNOWTH

A VISIT TO IRELAND'S VALLEY OF THE KINGS

WERNER ANTPÖHLER

MERCIER PRESS

Published in 2000 by
Mercier Press, PO Box 5
5 French Church Street Cork
Tel: (021) 427 5040; Fax (021) 427 4969
E-mail: books@mercier.ie
16 Hume Street Dublin 2
Tel: (01) 661 5299; Fax: (01) 661 8583
E-mail: books@marino.ie

First published in German in 1997 as
Newgrange, Dowth Und Knowth

Trade enquiries to CMD Distribution
55A Spruce Avenue
Stillorgan Industrial Park
Blackrock County Dublin
Tel: (01) 294 2556; Fax: (01) 294 2564
E-mail: cmd@columba.ie

© Werner Antpöhler 2000
Translation © Leonore Fischer 2000
Drawings © Lotti Antpöhler
Watercolours: Regine Bartsch © Lotti
Antpöhler
Photography © Werner Antpöhler, Fred
Hageneder
Design: Dragon Design GB

ISBN 1 85635 317 6

10 9 8 7 6 5 4 3 2 1

A CIP record for this title is available from the
British Library

Cover illustration by Michelle Conway
Cover design by Penhouse
Printed in Ireland by ColourBooks,
Baldoyle Industrial Estate, Dublin 13

Contents

Introduction

Everyone who travels around Ireland and visits the neolithic monuments of Newgrange, Dowth and Knowth in the 'Valley of the Kings' is impressed. 'But isn't the Valley of the Kings in Egypt?' the visitor might ask at first. Of course it is, but there is also a 'Valley of the Kings' here in Ireland in the north-west of Europe, and its awe-inspiring monuments were built before the Egyptian pyramids were ever begun.

Why were the massive megaliths of Newgrange, Dowth and Knowth built? For what purpose? What do the puzzling carvings on many of their stones mean?

We don't know for certain, since our ancestors left no records which would enable us to find rational answers for these questions. Our imagination is therefore the only means by which we can attempt to find explanations for the phenomena of Newgrange, Dowth and Knowth.

This book is designed to act as a companion to this attempt. It does not build data and facts into a scientific treatise but is descriptive, relating experiences in Ireland's 'Valley of the Kings'.

Over the years the author has travelled around Ireland, both privately and as a tour leader, and has visited the neolithic monuments of Newgrange, Dowth and Knowth many times. Two of these visits are described in this book. Personal experiences, ancient legends and personal interpretation are woven together here in such a way that the reader can easily follow in the author's footsteps.

Should the visitor come up with different interpretations than those presented in this book on viewing the megalithic monuments of Newgrange, Dowth and Knowth, so much the better! Great riddles can have many answers.

This book is intended to be both informative and attractive. It is hoped it will prepare the reader for a visit to the megalithic monuments of Newgrange, Dowth and Knowth and help to keep alive the memory of these immense, mysterious monuments for those who have been there!

Ex Oriente Lux – The Light Comes from the East

No one would deny that our occidental culture owes much to the Orient. Our basic religious and ethical beliefs originate in India and Persia, our knowledge of the heavens comes from the lands between the Tigris and Euphrates, and Egyptian physicians gave us much of our medical knowledge. And who can imagine what direction Western development might have taken without the philosophies of the Greeks! Truly, the light came from the east . . .

Only from the east? Surely our cultural development can't have been so one-sided. In Plato's legends of Atlantis we read that the Egyptian priests of Sais told Solon, the Greek philosopher, of a highly developed culture beyond the Pillars of Hercules, which is west of the Straits of Gibraltar in modern terms. The Egyptians had great respect for this powerful kingdom in the west, and called it Atlantis after the daughter of the god Atlas. They must have felt more than respect, for fear is audible in the priests' account and in their euphoric praises of Solon's Greek ancestors, whose heroic courage and warlike skill prevented the great power in the west from expanding. This left room for the development of the Egyptian culture we admire so much today.

So what lies behind this story of a great kingdom to the west of Gibraltar – Atlantis – and its people of the daughter of Atlas? Much has been written and debated on this topic. A very interesting and insightful contribution to this ongoing discussion has been made by the writer Helmut Tributsch in his book *Die Glaesernen Tuerme von Atlantis* (*The Glass Towers of Atlantis*).

Building on verifiable observations, Tributsch suggests that the legendary Atlantis of Plato was not destroyed, but still exists today as our Europe. For as Plato writes, concluding the Atlantis saga, 'Zeus, the god of gods . . . decided . . . however, to punish them [the inhabitants of Atlantis], that they might come to their senses and improve, not for punishment's sake.' So was there no destruction? No merciless extinction of the people of Atlantis, the daughter of Atlas? No disappearance (to carry on from Egyptian to Greek mythology) of the people of Europe, daughter of the Greek god Zeus, from the history of mankind?

So often we speak of the destruction of a culture and mean only that it faded away, to be replaced by another, and not necessarily that it was physically destroyed. This might have been the case for the megalithic culture which was perhaps the model for the myth of Atlantis in north-western Europe. Many historians and archaeologists believe that warlike invaders from the Near East landed on the coasts of Atlantic Europe between 2,000 and 1,000 years before we began reckoning time and that they gradually displaced the native populations and eventually overwhelmed them.

That Plato dramatised this historical replacement of one culture with another by converting it into a submergence myth should not surprise us, for the Atlantis story goes back to a time when people tended to think in pictorial rather than abstract form.

Anyone travelling today along the Atlantic coast between Morocco and the Orkney Islands will inevitably come across enormous and unusual stone monuments. Scientists have christened these monuments 'megaliths', which means 'great stones'. Our ancestors who erected these 'great stones' were part of what is known today as the megalithic culture, traces of which can be found everywhere along the Atlantic coasts of Europe. The

latest scientific calculations show that such monuments were built between 4,000 and 1,500 years before we began to calculate time, and are therefore, in part at least, older than the oldest pyramids of Egypt.

Were the Egyptian priests telling historical truth when they told Solon of Greece about the great civilisation beyond the Pillars of Hercules?

We know very little today about the history of Europe, because no written records of our ancestors survive – or at least none that we can read. However, a closer look will show that the people of the megalithic culture did leave some record of themselves behind, if only in the form of symbols. At Carnac, in the Gulf of Morbihan, at Stonehenge, on the Orkney Islands and in the Hebrides these records remain. Nowhere, however, are these stone records so clearly legible as at the megalithic site of Newgrange in Ireland.

Ex oriente lux
The light comes from the east?
Yes, but from the west as well.

First Visit to the 'Valley of the Kings'
December 1993

Newgrange: The Spiral Motifs of the Threshold

About 50 miles to the north of Dublin lies the Boyne Valley, the 'Valley of the Kings'. Here the kings and queens of the *Tuatha de Danaan*, the mythical invaders of Ireland, are supposed to have found their final resting places (see p 12). Newgrange is the best known of the three royal monuments Newgrange, Dowth and Knowth; its huge dome and facing of glittering quartzite draw the visitor under its spell even from afar. As we approach the entrance we find ourselves in front of a unique stone (see p 8/9), whose engraved pattern of spirals presents us with a veritable enigma.

> *Puzzling marks upon the stone*
> *Graven deep in its glowing blood.*

Thus did the German poet Novalis put his awe of such stones into words. Novalis was never in Ireland and never saw these mysterious carved spirals, but his verses may guide us as we attempt to unravel the message of these engraved figures. 'Graven deep in its glowing blood.' Blood lives. Are the spiral motifs in the stone of Newgrange trying to tell us something about life? About its coming and going? Why not? Goethe observed that plant growth follows a spiral pattern. He perceived that the unrolling spiral indicates growth and the rolling-up spiral suggests decay. Together growth and decay form life in its entirety. The symbol graven deep in the stone follows this pattern. Following the spirals

Valley of the Kings

Dublin

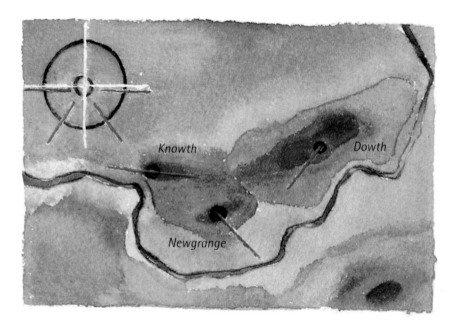

Knowth

Dowth

Newgrange

on the entrance stone of Newgrange clockwise, one sees that those on the left are rolling up or decreasing, whereas those on the right are unrolling or increasing images. How perplexing! A good reason to pause a little before the stone. This is obviously the first message of the stone: that we should pause. Not for nothing is the stone called the 'threshold stone'. 'He who crosses this threshold enters a Stone Age house of God' say artists, astronomers and spiritually motivated observers, supporting their view with myths which, although ancient, still live in Ireland today.

Let us stand a little longer at the threshold of the puzzle and hear how the myths explain it . . . The Dagda, the good god, lived in *Brú na Bóinne* (Newgrange). The *Brú* (palace) had previously belonged to Elcmar and Boand, the personification of the River Boyne. But the Dagda lured Elcmar away from his palace for a day, and then, by virtue of his magical powers, extended this one day to nine months. The result was a son born to Boand and the Dagda. His mother named him Oengus (the Youth), and explained this with the words, 'Young is the son conceived at dawn and born between morning and evening.' For this reason Oengus appears to us in Celtic mythology as the personification of the day. When Oengus had grown up, he went to his father, the Dagda, to demand a palace of his own. 'I have none for you,' the Dagda replied. But Oengus would not give up: 'Then give me leave to use your palace for a day and a night.' This the Dagda granted, and when the day and night had passed, he reminded Oengus that his time was up. But Oengus had outwitted his father. 'Day and night are a whole, an indivisible unit, an entity which cannot be measured by time. And it is this indivisible and incalculable day and night which you have granted me. The palace therefore belongs to me.' This is not completely irrelevant as a story. At any rate the palace is referred to subsequently more often as *Brú na Oengus* than as *Brú na Bóinne.*

What this myth tells us is fascinating. It describes the good god and the young Oengus, and contains images of day, dawn, conception, birth and permanence rather than old age or death. And the one time night is mentioned, it is in the context of the day, for 'day and night are an indivisible unity' – a whole only when seen together. Does the myth contain the same message as the deeply engraved, mysterious carvings on the threshold stone?

It is impossible to say for sure. But Newgrange can scarcely be described as an ordinary grave site. Why should death, of all things, have been glorified by such an enormous construction? When human life was so short, why would hundreds of workers, technicians and artists have exerted their time and energy simply so that death could be revered?

With these questions in mind, let us leave our enigmatic threshold stone for the present and walk around the walls of the enormous megalith of Newgrange.

Circuit of the Monument

In walking around the monument we travel in a circle. This circle is marked by seventy-nine uncut stones whose technical function is to ensure that the enormous dome of earth and stone does not collapse. But the number 79 is interesting from a numerological perspective, since if we take the number 79 apart and add the numbers 7 and 9, we get 16, which is double the number 8, and thus in symbolic language infinity doubled.

Our circuit could begin or end with any of the stones; and yet such a circuit always has the feeling of endlessness. This is not just a feeling, though, because a circle is infinite, having neither beginning nor end, and is therefore a symbol of eternity and of perpetual motion.

Reflecting on this, we notice that one of the great retaining stones is engraved with an almost identical pattern of spirals to the one that we saw on the threshold stone. This cannot be a coincidence. Moreover, by drawing an imaginary line from this stone to the threshold stone (see p 16), we connect two symbols which stand directly opposite one another. We discover simultaneously that this imaginary line from the threshold stone to its partner on the other side falls exactly along the passage leading into the interior of *Brú na Bóinne*.

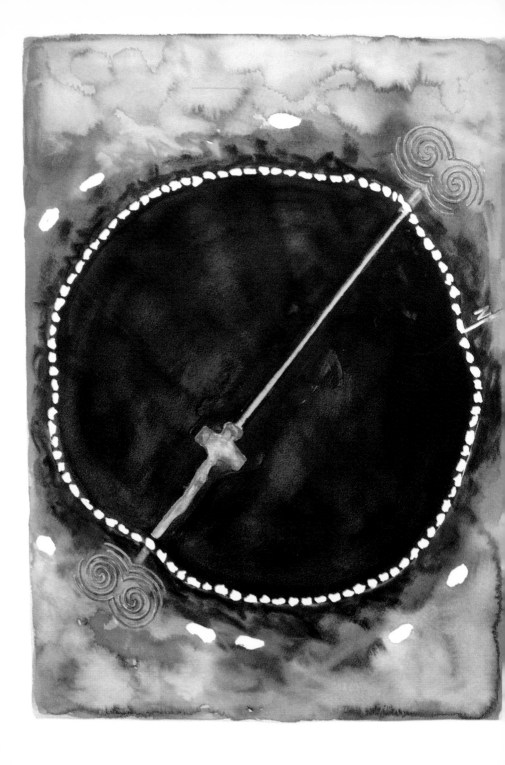

Unlike the circle, a line has a beginning and an end. It can therefore be a symbol of limitation. A symbol for the inevitable ending of all life as well, perhaps? A symbol of death? This interpretation is very appealing. But – to come back to our Celtic myth – Dagda is the *good* god, Oengus is the eternal *youth*; ending and death do not fit in here. And the stones at which our imaginary line terminates are the stones that are deeply carved with spiral motifs. Round and round the spirals move: rolling up and rolling out, falling asleep and awakening, inhaling and exhaling. Birth and death, winter and summer, sunrise and sunset . . . the circle has no beginning and no end, for all apparent beginnings and endings repeat themselves in a continuous rhythm, and thus again describe a circle, the symbol of eternity.

Perhaps that is the message *Brú na Bóinne* is telling us in its symbolism and construction – perhaps.

Michael O'Kelly Experiences the Winter Solstice

As long as we stay outside we can only observe and ponder. We must also prepare ourselves for what happens within. There, in the interior of the monument, the secret of *Brú na Bóinne* is protected like the kernel guarded inside the hard stone of a fruit.

The myths demonstrate, as the local people have always known, that a mystery cannot be unravelled logically. It will reveal itself if we know where to look.

Generations of archaeologists, in their attempt to explore the secrets of Newgrange, started by concentrating on excavation and analysis. This was to change in 1969, for Professor Michael O'Kelly had listened to what the local people had to say. 'At the winter solstice the rising sun sends its first rays straight into the rear chamber of *Brú na Bóinne*.' Michael O'Kelly, himself an archaeologist, laid aside his spade and books; on 21 December he came and stood within the innermost chamber of *Brú na Bóinne*, surrounded by nothing but darkness. He had squeezed through a passage 20 metres long, presumably pausing to try to interpret the cryptic carvings on the stones to the left and right of the passage. Knowing that thousands of tons of stone and earth loomed over him, he waited for the secret to reveal itself, and reveal itself it did. At 8.58 the sun rose over the horizon. Seconds later, it sent its first rays through the slit in the stone – the 'roof box' – over the palace entrance and right up into the farthest chamber of the great megalithic site of Newgrange.

What had happened? At the turn from winter to summer the sun had apparently reached the end of its course. Was this also the end of all life? Or would the sun turn and travel back, observing the law of perpetual regeneration? These may have been the fears of mankind 5,000 years ago, when *Brú na Bóinne* was built.

Michael O'Kelly knew that there was no reason to be afraid. He observed how the sun, which had followed him through the long, dark corridor, threw its rays onto the farthest altar stone of *Brú na Bóinne*'s central chamber. Lugh, the Celtic sun-god, had stretched his finger out and written on the cavernous dark:

Let there be light!

But that was not all; Lugh's finger not only touched the altar stone. The sun's light moved, it *turned*, and left Michael O'Kelly behind in darkness. Invisible outside in the light of day, here, in the cavernous dark, the movement was reduced to essentials, and yet magically magnified, so that it could not escape observation. The turning: the winter solstice!

Years later, others took the road to Newgrange – Martin Brennan and Tim O'Brien, for example. Following in Michael O'Kelly's footsteps, they were able to build upon his observations and capture the experience with quality cameras. Even sceptics were astonished by what they observed: the light of the sun, Lugh's finger, not only finds its way into the central chamber of the holy place every year on 21 December; even outside, in front of the entrance, it proclaims the message: The solstice comes!

19

Solar Hymn: Poem by Ingeborg Bachmann

About 15 metres from the threshold of the palace entrance stands a large, unworked stone. Shining across this, the rising sun throws its shadow upon the threshold stone in such a way that the spiral motifs of the threshold stone's left side exist only in a shadow world, so to speak, while the almost identical spirals of the right side shine brightly in the moving light of the rising sun. To the left, in shadow, the spirals roll up, contracting; to the right, bathed in sunlight, they unfurl, expanding (see p 20/21). Outside, in front of the entrance to the central mystery, the sun is its own herald, proclaiming the message: Light! Growth! Life!

Inside, in the inner sanctum of the holy place, it fulfils the promise it announced outside. Directed by cunningly placed standing stones and restricted to a narrow shaft of light, the rays of the sun find their way down the passage – roughly 20 metres long – to the central chamber at its end. Suddenly it is filled with the light of day; darkness must flee: 'Let there be light!'

Poets of all cultures and all ages have sung hymns to the sun, among them Ingeborg Bachmann, a German poet who died too young:

Lovelier than the revered moon and its
Lordly light,
Lovelier than the stars,
Famous medals of the night.
Far lovelier than the fiery appearance
Of a comet
And called to far lovelier things
Than any other heavenly body,
Since your life and my life
Depend every day upon it
Is the sun.

People may have praised the sun in this way over 5,000 years ago on 21 December, when, appearing to stand still, it fulfilled its promise: 'Let there be light again!'

But our ancestors did not content themselves with hymns of praise. In Newgrange they left us a genuine temple of the sun in which, on 21 December and on a few days before and after that date, we can experience the wonder of the winter solstice year after year. As long as . . . we have an invitation.

Invitation to the Celebration of the Winter Solstice

December 1993

I had just such an invitation, and this is how I managed to get it. Over the years Newgrange had become familiar to me, as I was there several times a year, sometimes as an ordinary visitor, sometimes as a leader with a group.

Again and again the monument itself had drawn me under its spell with its ingenious construction and the puzzling symbols on its colossal stones. Besides the information provided by the guides on site, I had collected pretty much all the available literature about it. Only one thing was lacking – the experience of the Newgrange mystery itself. At first this lack only affected my own personal interest in Newgrange. However, when I began to give illustrated lectures on the megalithic culture, Newgrange played a major part in these, and I could no longer be content to describe what I had heard about it – I wanted to experience Newgrange. But in order to be invited to Newgrange for the solstice one must be a VIP, which, unfortunately, I was not. So I wrote to the Office of Public Works, the government department in Dublin which is responsible for Newgrange. 'My dear and always friendly Irish people', I began in my attempt to persuade them, 'for years I have been coming to Newgrange, and as of last year I have been presenting illustrated lectures about the winter solstice in Newgrange. Can you imagine how embarrassing it is for me to talk about something I have never myself experienced? Please make me a VIP and send me an invitation to the winter solstice.' I had not long to wait for the answer. I had become a VIP overnight and I had been invited: I was delighted! But a closer look at the wording of the invitation had a sobering effect: 'You are cordially invited to the winter solstice of 1999.' Was this a joke? This was in the summer of 1993. I would have to wait six years to experience the solstice. I would simply have to come to terms with not being a VIP. A couple of months later, I began writing a book on Ireland. By the time I came to the chapter on Newgrange, the calendar had rushed on to October 1993. It was then that I had a brilliant idea. 'My dear and always friendly Irish people,' I faxed the Office of Public Works in Dublin, 'you have invited me to Newgrange for December 1999. Many thanks for this friendly evidence of goodwill. I am writing a book on Ireland and have just begun the chapter on Newgrange, yet now I discover to my own great shame that I am about to relate to my reader something about which I myself know only from reading . . . Please have pity on me and put forward your invitation to this year.' Thankfully the 'dear and always friendly' Irish had pity on my plight and faxed back that very day: 'You are invited to Newgrange on 19 December 1993. We meet at 8.30 on the site.'

It was October. Only a few weeks remained until December, and they flew by as though on wings. I used the time to revise everything I had read on Newgrange.

At last the time came to depart: on 16 December I flew to Dublin. Late that afternoon I arrived at the Boyne Valley Hotel in Drogheda, very close to Newgrange, and settled in for the next few days.

Now a period of impatient waiting began. In order to pass the time until the 19th, I visited various monuments in the Boyne Valley. This 'Valley of the Kings' is really an open-air museum, containing Slane, where St Patrick is supposed to have committed the sacrilege of lighting the Easter fire before the High King; Monasterboice, with its well-preserved Celtic crosses; and Mellifont Abbey, whose ruins call to mind the transition from Celtic to Roman Christianity.

The weather was changeable, and the sun could only show itself occasionally. What would the weather be like on the morning of 19 December? All other questions took second place to this, because the sun would only show itself on the morning of 19 December if the skies were clear, and only then could the 'miracle of Newgrange' come to pass.

I had got through all the waiting quite well up to this point, but now my nerves were on edge.

On 19 December, the day of my invitation, I woke up in the morning on German time – in other words, very, very early. By 6.00 I was pacing up and down the hall. The night porter watched me out of the corner of his eye and with a look of concern finally asked, 'Are you not feeling well?' 'Oh yes, I am feeling well, it's just that I am terribly nervous because . . .' and I gave him the full story of how I came to be invited to Newgrange. He drew up a stool for me by the hearth, where tongues of fire were already licking up. 'I'll start by getting you some tea and toast.' The tea took effect, and my head and stomach settled themselves. Then the night porter had some solid comfort to offer. 'Calm yourself. The wind changed in the night from south to north-east. It's a chilly day out, with a clear sky. Rest assured, the sun will show, and you will experience your miracle. I know what I'm talking about, I grew up near Newgrange.'

I headed off at about 7.00 and reached Newgrange within half an hour. Everything was still mantled in the grey light of dawn. Only the quartzite-veneered facade of the great mound of Newgrange loomed whitely in the dark surroundings. Moment by moment the dark receded into the endless night and suddenly a pale streak appeared in the east: the day was here! And what a day! Within minutes the heavens were illuminated with green, yellow and pink light.

The first cars rolled up. People climbed out in silence. They were all VIPs like me . . . Clare Tuffy from the Office of Public Works came to guide us into the sanctuary. I had known her for years. 'Aren't you lucky!' she called out to me. At last, we were standing before the threshold stone of *Brú na Bóinne*, the solar temple whose origins lie hidden in the mists of time. Our guide made the requisite introductory speech, casting glances back over her shoulder every so often so as not to miss anything happening on the eastern horizon. Everything remained just as it had been, bright with the day – red, fiery red. Our guide's face was just as radiant as the sky. She was clearly delighted that in a few moments she would be able to reveal a true miracle to the eighteen impatient visitors, the two previous days having been utter failures, with overcast skies.

And now it begins . . . One by one we push our way up the 20 metres or so of the passage, passing the colossal upright stones on the left and right, with their familiar symbolic carvings. After two or three minutes we are all gathered in the central chamber of the sanctuary. Our guide goes back to the entrance, casts a critical look at the eastern sky, returns and switches off her torch. We stand in darkness, in the utter blackness of a cave. Some of us mutter a few words, then all is silence. Everyone waits tensely for the 'miracle of the winter solstice'. And the miracle occurs.

Suddenly in the darkness a ray of light appears at our feet, as if it had been fired from the string of a bow. Silvery-white, it seems no bigger than an arrowhead. And now we witness a drama which can scarcely be described in words. The arrowhead moves: clockwise along the stones on the left side of the sanctuary. From one minute to the next it grows, becoming as long as a spear and changing colour from silvery white to deep orange, bathing the central chamber right up to the capstone 6 metres above us in gliding light. Where everything had been utterly dark around us before, now we can all see each other clearly, and we follow our guide's gesture as she points to a stone on the right side of the rear chamber: 'There!'

As an image in the theatre is produced magically out of the background by lighting effects, so the spiral motif suddenly appears, graven deep at eye level in one of the massive blocks of stone, this time in triple form. Coming, Staying, Going: is that the meaning of this message?

Logically we know that the ray of light playing though the chamber of the palace is caused by the movement of the sun along its course outside, but the miracle occurring before our eyes suppresses all thought for the moment. There is no time for thought anyway, for now the second act of the drama begins: our spear of light has nearly touched the rear stone of the chamber and already now it turns to recede. As though guided by an unseen hand, it begins to return along the right wall of the central chamber. Our guide sighs a soft 'that was it,' and she is right. It has occurred: The sun's turning, the winter solstice.

The instant that the orange spear of light comes close to touching the farthest stone of the sanctum of Newgrange, it announces that everything will continue as normal. This passage from left to right, from breathing in to breathing out, from winter to summer, occurs so quietly that, hypnotised by the ghostly spear of light, we almost fail to notice it. In complete silence the spear of light turns and retreats, touching the stones with their puzzling, deeply carved designs on the right wall. It becomes shorter and paler every minute. Suddenly it is only the size of an arrowhead. It turns silvery-white – and it is gone.

Our guide switches her torch on again. No one speaks; we are

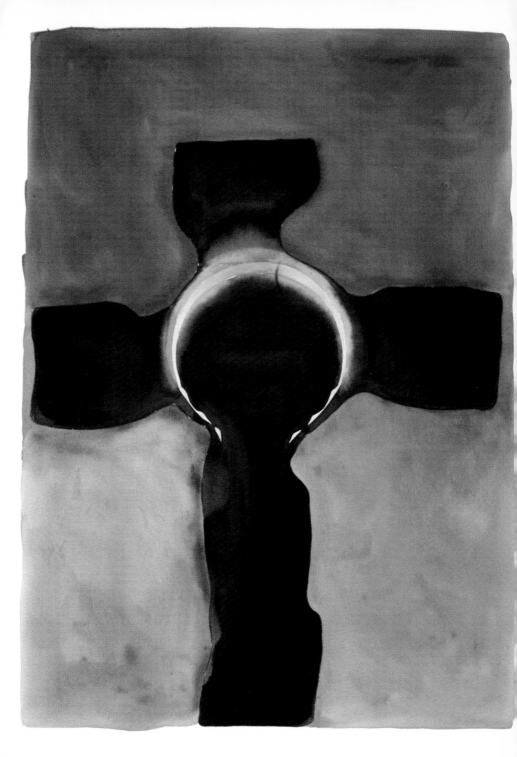

overawed and dumbstruck with wonder. In silence we return along the passage. Only the deep carvings on the mighty stones that line both sides of the passage speak, and then only in their own mysterious language. Then the modern world possesses us again and we stand outside in the bright light of 19 December 1993. Unheeding, the sun pursues its path, or rather (to call to mind Galileo's teaching) the Earth quietly continues its circuit round the sun.

I had expected that we, the eighteen 'chosen ones', would gather together afterwards for an exchange of ideas, but nothing of the sort happened. I heard only the slamming of car doors as everybody made their own way off.

Once again I stood sunk in thought on the spot where I had often stood before in front of the threshold stone with its spiral motifs. The shadow which the megalith had recently thrown over the left spiral had shortened, and now it barely touched the lower edge of the threshold stone. Both halves of the spiral motifs were now bathed in brilliant sunlight.

That which I had experienced lay behind me: a cruciform chamber in which the travelling light of the sun had described a circle. For a few moments the near-perfect cross shape (the symbol of matter) and the light of the sun (the symbol of the spirit) had fused into an unforgettable mandala. Even today the elements of the sun and cross form the basis of the Celtic Cross.

32

Poem Remembering Newgrange

The winding spiral draws a graphic rhyme
So wondrous in its waving convolution
On venerable slab of bleaching stone,
What may their meaning be? Do they intone
Some magic chant, some mystical delusion
Persisting from some superstitious time?

You seek to find some trivial explanation
Of ciphers written in some unsophisticated day?
Seek on – the riddles tell
No tales of facile confirmation
Before you will be blown away
By breath of time – for you as well
In spirals swing through time, expanding into life,
Now standing bright in brilliant light
To shrink away when troubles take their toll
To sink into the shadows of your soul.

Coming and going,
Shrinking and growing
While light and shadow, twining into rhyme
Go tumbling through infinities of time.

Werner Antpöhler

Dowth: Associations with the Newgrange Myth

The day was still young; the sun had moved southwards and now stood high and warm in the heavens. The year was nearly at an end; winter waited at the door. What should I do with myself for the rest of the day? Drive straight to Dublin? No, the Boyne Valley had too much to offer: nearby were the megalithic sites of Dowth and Knowth, which are, in a sense, the sisters of Newgrange.

In driving back to the main Drogheda–Slane road I would have to pass Dowth anyway. I stopped the car and tramped back through soggy fields, pushing my way through prickly gorse, and eventually emerged to stand in front of – disappointment. So this was the megalithic site of Dowth! The entrance to the monument *was* visible, but I could not go in, because it had been blocked up with iron bars. Obviously the archaeologists had laid spade and enthusiasm aside and secured the entrance in order to prevent inquisitive visitors from having a look inside before they did. Here at Dowth, as at Newgrange, a threshold stone lies before the entrance. But in comparison with the artistic spiral symbolism of Newgrange, the Dowth stone seems understated. And yet the symbols carved in this stone must also have had some meaning. A circle with twelve rays might indicate a division of the year into twelve months, and one with eight rays might mark the eight main positions of the sun. It is possible that it could mean that. But we don't know for sure. Perhaps 5,000 years ago there were contemporary concerns and beliefs which wholly elude us today, but which our ancestors regarded as important enough to be eternalised in stone.

I recalled what I had read of Dowth in books. Dowth is only

about half the size of Newgrange, but it is by no means less significant. While Newgrange captures the sunrise on the winter solstice, Dowth captures the sunset on the same day. Even the myths link Dowth with the remarkable story of Newgrange.

The druid Bresal had taken it into his head to build a tower whose tip would reach the heavens, but he could only hire the workers he needed for one day. His sister came to his aid by magically halting the sun in the sky until the work was finished. But Bresal committed incest with his sister, which negated her magical powers and caused the sun to set too soon. As the myth relates, 'Darkness overcame her.'

'This place shall forever be called darkness,' Bresal's sister lamented, and so it came to pass: to the present day the light of the sunset falling into Dowth at the winter solstice reminds us of the longest night and of the longest dark period of the year. Newgrange and Dowth belong together like day and night, light and dark, sunrise and sunset.

With this knowledge I climbed into the car again and drove away. I had driven a few miles along the road towards Slane when a sign by the road advertising 'teas and coffees' reminded me that other than the piece of toast provided by the friendly night porter in the hotel, my stomach was empty. The tea shop was a small one; I had just decided to leave again when the woman behind the counter addressed me with an encouraging 'Isn't it a beautiful day!' And *what* a beautiful day! Beautiful for the woman in the tea shop because a radiant winter sun graced us with light and warmth, and beautiful for me because I had experienced Newgrange. I had to tell her of my great adventure. The woman listened, but seemed unmoved, as if to say, 'So what?' I was annoyed. Wasn't there more to say than that? But then, while showing me through a side door to a nicely set table in the good room, she recalled that as children the locals had always run to Newgrange around Christmas time 'to catch the sun'! I perked up.

So the local inhabitants had always known that Newgrange is not really a grave in its strictest sense, but more a solar temple. Yet still we speak of passage graves when talking of the colossal megalithic sites of Western Europe. Old habits die hard! But now that the friendly countrywoman spoke of 'catching the sun', I was more convinced than ever that Newgrange is not a mausoleum – it is a temple of the sun!

Knowth: A Brief Visit

Since I was in the Boyne Valley, I drove around to Knowth as well – the third of the great monuments on the River Boyne. But here I found a great bustle: the archaeologists were employing heavy machinery and Knowth looked like a construction site. I could only stand at a distance and look over at the western entrance of this overwhelming megalithic site. I knew from books that it was designed, 5,000 years ago, so that at the equinoxes of March and September the sun would leave its unmistakable message, as it does at Newgrange and Dowth. In the morning it sends its first rays up the eastern passage of the monument, and in the evening it bids farewell with its last light by illuminating the western passage, before night covers all with darkness.

It seemed a pity that I could not explore the solar temple of Knowth, but the archaeological director would not take responsibility for my safety in view of the dangers of construction sites.

It didn't matter. For today I was happy and content, having experienced the miraculous trick of the sun at Newgrange. But great experiences must be digested quietly, and where in the Boyne Valley would one find a better place than in the bar of the Conyngham Arms Hotel in Slane?

Here, where over the years archaeologists of note and fame have argued over facts and theses, I pulled myself up to the turf fire as a snail pulls itself into its shell. What with the enigmatic speech of symbols and the magnificent miracle of the sun, there was a great deal to think about.

Second Visit to the 'Valley of the Kings'
September 1996

Knowth: General Impressions

Nearly three years had passed since my experience of the miracle at Newgrange. In the meantime I had accompanied several tours to Ireland and show them 'my' Newgrange.

Now in September 1996, I was in the Boyne Valley again, in the 'Valley of the Kings'. I knew that the equinox would fall on the 22nd and that the miracle would occur at Knowth at both sunrise and sunset.

But 'there will be no special celebration on 22 September' the Office of Public Works responded, when, at the beginning of September, I begged to be invited to the celebration of the equinox. So, no solar miracle at Knowth. I had to accept this, but I was not happy about it. 'One never knows,' I said to myself, and so on the afternoon of 19 September, I made my way to the entrance to Knowth despite the written refusal from Dublin. Filled with expectation, I purchased my entrance ticket just like any other visitor, entered, and was disappointed. Knowth was still a construction site! Directly before my eyes, some 50 metres from the western chamber, where at sunset in a few hours the miracle of Knowth would occur, a high metal fence made it unmistakably plain that I was not welcome. What now? 'I will just have to content myself with photographing the enormous erratics [rocks that have been transported from their place of origin] which surround the foot of Knowth's huge dome,' I told myself. An alluring task, for the great mound of Knowth is bordered by roughly 120 erratics, of which about 90 are decorated with symbols and ornaments. So I joined a group of visitors. After just a few steps our guide came to a halt by the first of the great boundary stones. She commented on its puzzling decorations, but then she began to explain other stones, both with and without symbols, using photos and sketches from a book. The reason for this was obvious: most of the kerb stones mentioned in the literature lay behind the construction fence and, moreover, were covered with black plastic sheeting. This was a bitter disappointment indeed! I went back to the hut where I had bought my entrance ticket and voiced my dismay. All to no avail. 'The fence is there because the archaeologists must work undisturbed,' I was told. And 'Just imagine if the kerb stones were not covered up, and were exposed to the abrasive dust and rubble of the earth-moving equipment! Why, the damage done to the decorations engraved some 5,000 years ago would be irreparable!'

The young girl who appeased me in this fashion was right, of course. And when I was told that I could purchase copies of slides and photographs from the Office of Public Works archives at any time, I calmed down. And hadn't these culturally unique stones lain for nearly 5,000 years under rubble until the archaeologists took their spades to them in the 1960s? Who was I, that I should have to photograph the kerb stones on this particular day of all days – 19 September 1996.

Borrowing a book by Professor George Eogan, the famous chief archaeologist of Knowth, from the hut, I stood for a while at the site. The book describes how systematic excavations of Knowth have been going on since 1962. The results, presented with photos and drawings, read like an adventure story.

'We're closing up now,' came a voice from behind me. I had been engrossed in the photographs and drawings. It was indeed nearly 6 o'clock – how time flies. Did people 5,000 years ago conceive of time as movement? Probably not – not as a linear progression divided up into past-present-future, at least. Time, for them, was probably bound into a cyclical, constantly repeating rhythm – or so it is depicted symbolically on many of the stones, at any rate. Time was probably not yet 'lost' or 'gained.' That evening in the Conyngham Arms Hotel in Slane I read *The Stars and the Stones* by Martin Brennan. If Professor George Eogan's official book on Knowth is like an archaeological adventure, then one might say that Martin Brennan's book actually is an adventure in places. One gets goose-flesh when reading about how Martin Brennan climbed over the fence of Knowth on a foggy night and how he then saw that on the day of the autumnal equinox the shadow of a menhir thrown by the setting sun upon the threshold stone of the western passage coincided exactly with the pronounced vertical line of the decoration. It was this very phenomenon that I too had wanted to observe. It was for this very reason that I had come! But nothing now could come of that: I had no wish to emulate Martin Brennan.

Next morning I was at the site again, this time with two companions: Professor George Eogan's book and Martin Brennan's. I leafed through both books, comparing photos and drawings, and looking from time to time through the fence over to the plastic-covered kerb stones so vividly described in both books. I had to laugh at my own situation – I had never visited a museum or art gallery in this way before!

Knowth is enormous: from east to west it measures some 80 metres in diameter by 95 metres from north to south. With a height of 10 metres, the entire building comprises an area of around 6000 square metres. In all, around 120 kerb stones surround the edge of the mound; of these, around 90 bear symbolic ornament.

In the interior of this gigantic mound, two passages, 34 and 40 metres in length respectively, lead to the palace chambers within. And again inside there is a wealth of colossal stones with mysterious symbology. Even the barest plan conveys how powerful and impressive the megalithic site of Knowth is. In a few years,

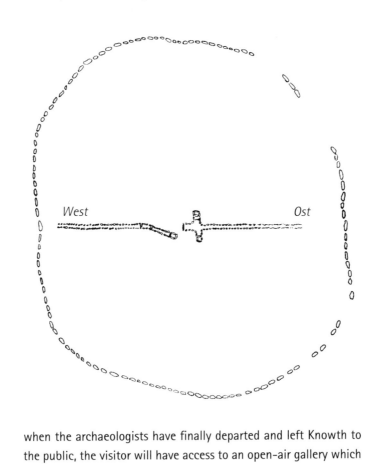

when the archaeologists have finally departed and left Knowth to the public, the visitor will have access to an open-air gallery which is so far unrivalled in terms of size and quality. Even now, with only a fraction of the majestic site available to admire, Knowth is fascinating.

The questions which repeatedly arise upon viewing the symbols and ornaments upon the kerb stones are: What might these signs mean? Do they have something to tell modern man?'

To answer these questions we must start with a more basic one: What are we dealing with here – ornament or symbol? *The Oxford English Dictionary* defines 'ornament' as: 'a thing used or serving to adorn, decoration to embellish a building (from Latin *ornamentum*, equipment).' For 'symbol' it states: 'a thing conventionally regarded as typifying, representing or recalling something especially an idea or quality; mark or character, taken as the conventional sign of some object, idea function or process. (Gr *symbolon*, mark, token)' Bringing these explanations from the modern conceptual world to bear upon the ciphers from the neolithic era, the engravings upon the enormous stones of the megalithic culture must be symbols and not ornaments. For it would be completely illogical to assume that our ancestors transported these stone colossi such long distances simply to 'embellish' them. It makes more sense if they regarded them as 'representing or recalling something', as a 'sign of some idea or process.'

Today we must look for the meaning lying behind the symbols; we must search in dictionaries for conceptual definitions. Five thousand years ago it may have been enough for wise priests to take their novices for a meditative walk around the mound, merely showing them the engraved symbols at each individual station or stone. There was probably an immeasurably greater gap between priests (the knowing) and novices (the unknowing) in the neolithic era than there is today between teacher and student. The symbol – a condensed expression of relationships – may have served to bridge this gap. It is quite possible that students in the Stone Age could understand the complex concepts behind such a symbol as quickly and comprehensively as we grasp the headlines of a newspaper. Thus the symbol may simply have served as a medium for communication between teachers and their students 5,000 years ago.

Let us imagine ourselves before some of the kerb stones and ask yet again: What might these symbols mean? What are they trying to tell us?

Neolithic Symbology, Explained through Four Examples

Example 1: The Threshold Stones at the Two Entrances of Knowth

Both entrance stones bear symbolic decorations, but over and above this they carry out a 'technical' function with respect to the tall, narrow stones placed, in both cases, a few metres away. As in Newgrange, the sun throws the shadow of the standing stone upon the threshold. Descriptions by those who have observed and photographed this event indicate that on the day of the equinox, that is, on 20 March and 22 September, this shadow falls exactly upon the pronounced vertical line of the given threshold stone; at the eastern passage at sunrise, at the western passage at sunset.

The kerb stones immediately adjacent to the two threshold stones bear symbols as well, both having seven arcuate lines. Seven is the holy number, for if three represents the spiritual, and four the material world, then seven is the sum of both. This symbol on the two stones may therefore bear the message, 'Here on this threshold stone the opposition between spiritual and material, day and night, is resolved. All opposites are brought into healing or holy balance. It is the equinox, when day and night are equal.

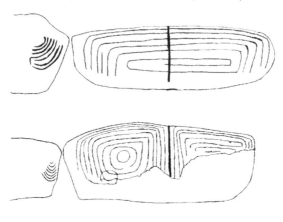

Example 2: Kerb Stone 12 (West Entrance, Facing North)

I recognised this stone in the books at once. Only the day before, I had actually stood in front of it, for it is outside the fence. The message of the engraved symbols is simple – or so it seems; in any case it is very marked. Four flattened ovals of about the same size make up the 'face' of this kerb stone. The stone is unquestionably trying to tell us something about the number four. The four seasons? That spring, summer, autumn and winter are equal in the yearly rhythm? Is this why the ovals are of approximately equal size and of roughly the same artistic design? It could be that; it seems it really must be that. And then there is the marked horizontal line between the two upper and lower ovals. Horizontal – bringing things into balance. If this figure is to be read in this way, then it expresses symbolically what the threshold stones show functionally: the equinox, when day and night are equal.

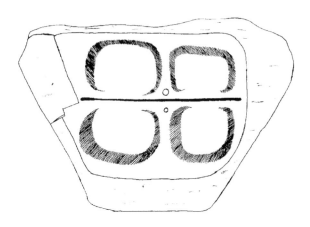

Example 3: Sacrificial Stone Basin (in the Right Chamber of the Eastern Passage)

Circles, arcs and lines are all we can make out of the decorations on this stone. A second look, however, reveals a system – a numerical order. Circles or arcs appear four times; the line is engraved twelve times. The four: could this represent the four cardinal positions of the sun, the four seasons once again? And the twelve: doesn't this suggest the twelve months? This idea becomes a near-certainty when we look a third time at the stone and its decoration. The stone itself is circular in form and a circular figure (the arc) is shown four times. The circle is eternal, as is our concept of the sun. Is the shape of the stone, therefore, and the four-fold circular engraving, a symbol of the sun? It may well be, especially as the circle (the sun) is carved above the line (the lunar cycle) and thus dominates it.

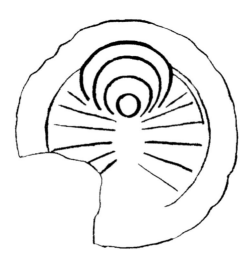

Example 4: The Ghostly Guardian

'Then, coming to a stone sill, we illuminated the orthostat on its inner right side and beheld what seemed to be an anthropomorphic figure with two large, staring eyes. This ghostly guardian suggested that we were approaching the inner sanctum.'

This extract from Professor George Eogan's book *Knowth* describes some of his adventures during the archaeologists' investigation of the western entrance.

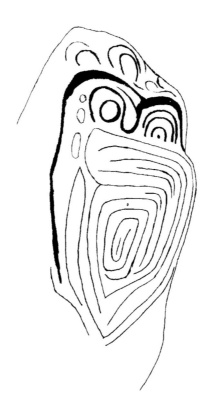

Professor Eogan's description of this stone as a 'ghostly guardian' expresses the spontaneous reaction of a first impression. Imagine: the entrance had finally been located but stones large and small lay in the way. A passage could be seen behind them. Tension was mounting, and then suddenly these 'large staring eyes' caught the torch's beam of light. It must have seemed like a guardian, set there to bar the way to intruders. Certainly the stone's shape resembles that of a human face – the 'large, staring eyes' remove all doubt. But is it a guardian? Are these eyes intended for us? Don't they give the opposite impression, that they look down into their own, speechless face? The face is entirely speechless, because it has neither mouth nor nose. 'In any case, the lack of a mouth is a sign that the organ which makes expression possible is irrelevant for people of magic. Understanding among the I-group, among the we, does not need speech, but takes place more or less . . . telepathically.' Perhaps with these words Jean Gebser, the great modern cultural philosopher, has given us a useful clue to understanding the megalithic time and its symbology. 'Magic is action without consciousness of watching,' Jean Gebser continues. But a guardian must be aware if he is to perform his task. Our 'guardian', however, does not speak (he has no mouth); he does not breathe (he has no nose); deeply sunk in self-contemplation, he meditates. On what does he meditate? Obviously on the symbol of the spiral, for the complete concentration of his 'large, staring eyes' is focused upon this symbol unrolling in spiral coils across his face.

The spiral! We encounter it so often in Newgrange, Dowth and Knowth. The spiral – symbol for growing and waning life.

Standing in front of the 'guardian' one sees in its symbology the watchman at the door, who guards a sacred area from the uninitiated. Anyone trained in symbology – the speech beyond space and time – is more inclined when meeting the guardian to think of a spiritual guide directing the visitor at the threshold of

the sanctuary toward the right way – the meditative way inwards. I gave the photograph of the guardian to our artist, Regine Bartsch, in Ireland and asked her to work up its symbolic message artistically in watercolour. Amazingly, the artist must have had the same impression of the stone that I have described here, since she emphasised both the spiral and the 'great, staring eyes' by using the dominant colour red without our ever having discussed the matter in advance.

Coda

Experts in various fields have presented the widest possible variety of ideas about megalithic 'art'; probably no one theory is the only right one. Although this may annoy us, it should not keep us from admiring unreservedly this unique artwork of our Stone Age ancestors. Certainly we should not dismiss it as barbaric, as has been done even quite recently.

'Art does not try to portray the visible but to reveal the invisible,' Paul Klee commented once, when those who were trying to recognise something familiar in his pictures found their accustomed frames of reference inadequate.

Newgrange: Lintel Stone with Eight Lozenges

It was Saturday 21 September. My accommodation in Dublin was booked from Sunday the 22nd. I could stay another whole day in the Boyne Valley, so I stayed. Should I just look at Newgrange again, I wondered. Twenty minutes later I was there. If diggers and cranes commanded the scene at Knowth, at Newgrange it was the tourists. It is amazing how many people come from all over the world to see and experience for themselves the high degree of culture our ancestors of the New Stone Age attained!

I stationed myself before the entrance, and again my attention was immediately drawn to the spiral symbology on the threshold stone. The voice of the guide talking to a group of visitors seemed far away, but I could see him gesture towards the roof box over the entrance, probably explaining how the rising sun at the winter solstice sends its first rays through this opening. My gaze remained fixed on the lintel that lies over the roof box, with its engraved lozenges. I had often admired this decoration, but today I noticed for the first time that it consisted of eight lozenges (seven complete lozenges and a half one at each end). At the winter solstice, the rising sun greets a decoration of eight lozenges before illuminating the sanctuary – the palace itself. This lintel, with its decoration, must have a deeper meaning to offer us.

Are the eight lozenges of the lintel over the roof box intended to refer to astronomical phenomena, telling us that Newgrange is, in fact, a solar temple? If so, then there must be a meaning to the fact that each lozenge is vertically divided, giving us a total of sixteen decorative elements on the stone. We already met the number 16 when we walked round the mound, as the sum of the digits of the seventy-nine kerb stones. That makes one stop and think. It reminds us that some cultures are said to have used a calendar of sixteen units instead of the twelve-part lunar calendar. If we accept this as a cultural and historical phenomenon, then the megalithic culture of north-western Europe must have followed a solar calendar. So from this perspective also, Newgrange must have been a solar temple. What else could it be?

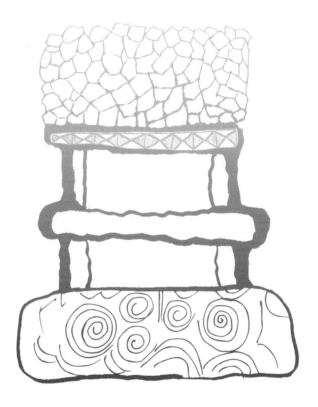

The important positions of the sun in the year are the two solstices (June and December), the two equinoxes (March and September) and the halfway points between these dates (February, May, August, November) – a total of eight cardinal points. The sketch on page 55 demonstrates how Newgrange marks the two solstices in the annual cycle, for both of these astronomical events are marked at their respective positions of sunrise and sunset by strikingly decorated stones.

I decided to do a circuit of the mound to check whether these famous kerb stones, with their familiar decoration, marked the positions of sunrise and sunset on the summer and winter solstice in reality as well as on our sketch.

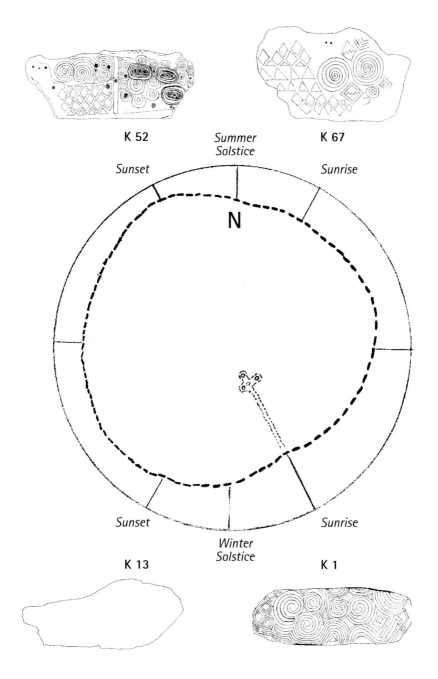

K 52

Summer
Solstice

K 67

Sunset

Sunrise

N

Sunset

Sunrise

Winter
Solstice

K 13

K 1

I knew of course that kerb stone K1 at the entrance marks the rising sun at the winter solstice. Kerb stone K52, exactly opposite K1, also lies exactly on the position of the setting sun at the summer solstice. The decorated stone K67 (rising sun at the summer solstice) again corroborates the sketch. But where was the stone that denotes the sunset of the winter solstice, marked as the counterpart of threshold stone K1? The stone was there, but no symbols were engraved upon it! I was vexed. Was the entire interpretation of the symbology going to turn out to be a wild theory? The ladies in the ticket hut helped me. 'Oh, but yes, K13 does indeed have the usual symbols.' I went back and walked along the kerbstones, counting them with care. K13 was there, but no symbols. 'I can still count, surely,' I thought, and returned to the ticket hut. The lady opened Professor O'Kelly's voluminous book on Newgrange. 'Here is K13, and *with* symbols. The symbols on this stone, however, are on the back, not visible to the viewer. Our archaeologists know that the symbolic drawings are present, however, because they measured and photographed the stone on all sides before replacing it in the position in which it was found.' This was informative, but was not a good enough explanation for me. 'Why were the symbols engraved on the side which could not be seen?' I wanted to know, and was answered by a helpless shrug of the shoulders. More questions came to my mind, though now I directed them at myself. Why go to so much trouble and effort, when afterwards the result will be concealed from the sight of the worshipper? Perhaps nothing concretely visible was to be worshipped? Perhaps the priests deliberately wanted their pupils to search for the unseen to test how far their abilities had developed in visualising such concepts? Perhaps they placed their novices at the threshold stone at sunrise on the morning of the winter solstice and explained the symbology of the spirals to them, and in the evening at kerb stone K13 tested them by asking, 'What do you see now? Can you construct the companion to the threshold stone of

Longest Day – 21 June

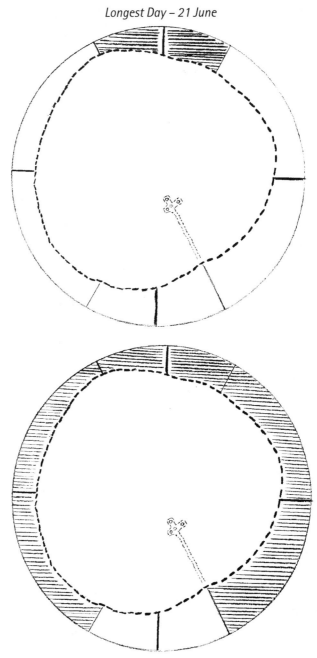

Longest Night – 21 December

this morning without being provided with the picture?'

This is more a conjecture than a thesis, yet didn't Goethe say 'nothing is inside, nothing is outside, for that which is inside, is outside.' The belief that opposites are complementary to each other, forming a whole between them, has clearly always existed. Why shouldn't priests and teachers of megalithic times have known this ancient wisdom and have taught it by contrasting seen and unseen symbols?

Final View: The Spiral Once Again

It had been a long day. I stood on the footbridge leading across the River Boyne to the big new visitors' centre. Like the waters of the Boyne swirling under me, the impressions of my many visits to the 'Valley of the Kings' swirled through my mind. Apart from the unforgettable experience of the winter solstice in Newgrange, it was the spiral symbol which repeatedly occupied my thoughts. And while I lingered on the bridge, lost in thought, I looked up at the great panoramic window of the new visitors' centre and saw the spiral itself on it, on an unprecedented scale. It is etched upon the glazing of the galleries so prominently as to give the impression that the meaning of the spiral must be more important than the meaning of any other of the symbols of Newgrange, Dowth or Knowth.

And really, what other symbol has as much energy as the spiral, for it represents the circle – the symbol of perfection – in continuous motion and development!

The spiral is to be found as a symbol in the art, literature and architecture of many cultures. This has been thoroughly documented by Jil Purce in her book *Die Spirale – Symbol der Seelenreise* (*The Spiral – Symbol of the Soul's Voyage*). She quotes the following lines by William Butler Yeats. He, great poet of the Irish, will have the last word in this book:

Jaunting, journeying

To his own dayspring

He unpacks the loaded pern —

Knowledge he shall unwind

Through victories of the mind.

From 'Shepherd and Goatherd'

Postscript:
Departure from the 'Valley of the Kings'

There is still so much more to be said about Newgrange, Dowth and Knowth – so much more to ask!

What I have written here is meant to show that the megalithic monuments of Ireland's 'Valley of the Kings' are not just impressive technical constructs, but that there are clearly messages encoded within their visible forms. Whether these messages are timeless – whether they still have something to say to us today – remains the main question.

One thing is sure: Newgrange, Dowth and Knowth are positioned in such a way that on these sacred sites the course of the sun can be observed and measured. It is no great leap to deduce from this that these three monuments together constitute a major solar observatory. Filling out these facts with colourful mythology and the cryptic language of symbology, as I have done here, makes it clear that we in Europe can be just as proud of our great spiritual heritage as the people of the Orient are of theirs.

Newgrange, Dowth and Knowth are far from having yielded up all their secrets. The archaeologists whose work and zealous research have given us so much will undoubtedly continue to mesmerise us with new discoveries.

We must continue to contemplate these secrets and to ask questions, for only those who ask questions get answers – if not today, then tomorrow. Newgrange, Dowth and Knowth will remain there for a long while yet and will surely continue to inspire our wholehearted admiration.

Sources

Bachman, Ingeborg. *An Die Sonne*. Piper, 1978.

Brennan, Martin. *The Stars and Stones*. London: Thames and Hudson, 1983.

The Concise Oxford English Dictionary, Ninth Edition. Oxford: Clarendon Press, 1995.

Eogan, George. *Knowth and the Passage Tombs of Ireland*. London: Thames and Hudson, 1986.

Gebser, Jean. *Ursprung und Gegenwart*. Munich: dtv Publishers, 1992.

Purce, Jil. *Die Spirale – Symbol der Seelenreise*. Munich: Kösel, 1988.

Tributsch, Helmut. *Die Gläsernen Türme von Atlantis*. Berlin: Ullstein Verlag.

The drawings in this book have been inspired by photographs taken by the author as well as some contained in the books *Newgrange*, *Knowth* and *The Stars and Stones* (all published by Thames and Hudson, London).